The
Ultimate Fan Book
TIK TOK FAMOUS

PHOTOS AND FACTS ABOUT THE NEXT GENERATION OF VIRAL SENSATIONS

Malcolm Croft

MORTIMER

CONTENTS

INTRODUCTION: GENERATION TIKTOK

WELCOME TO THE WONDERFUL WORLD OF TIKTOK – THE APP THAT *EVERYONE* TODAY IS TALKING ABOUT. IN 2020, TIKTOK HAS BECOME THE PLANET'S MOST POPULAR SOCIAL MEDIA PLATFORM FOR CREATORS OF ALL AGES, SHAPES AND SIZES. THEY COME TOGETHER TO MAKE QUICK BITE-SIZED CLIPS FOR HUNDREDS OF MILLIONS OF FANS TO LIKE, LOVE, LAUGH, SWIPE, SHARE AND, MOST IMPORTANTLY, RECREATE IN THEIR OWN ORIGINAL WAY.

TikTok is the place to be. It's home to the world's most brilliant, inventive, funny, weird, silly, smart (and often stupid, savage and outspoken) creators. It's perhaps the only place in the online world where people from all walks of life – chefs, athletes, comedians, dancers, movie-makers, musicians, singers, pranksters, philosophers, *anyone* – can come together under the same roof and share their passions with like-minded souls. *All at once, in sync.*

TikTok is the place where celebrity superstars can share their incredibly famous lives; a place where "ordinary" people can show off their extraordinary skills; a place where anyone, for better or worse, can speak their mind and scream at the top of their lungs; a place where art is appreciated and discovered; and, yes, a place where fame and fortune is just a swipe away. On TikTok, happiness can be found, and sadness can be shared. Trends are born and news is broken. Challenges are set. And met. It's a place of extreme positivity and, at times, devastating negativity. But, more importantly, it's a place where everyone is welcome and a place where those who like you will let you lead them. It is the place that 1.5 billion users call home, after all.

From Charli D'Amelio's choreography to Loren Gray's beauty tips, Zach King's special-effects wizardry to Jiff Pom's super doggy cuteness, and everything and everyone in between, TikTok is the future of social media today and it is here to stay. Because it is more than just an app. It is the home of the new breed of modern celebrity, the TikTok Famous – where stars are born every second. But, as much as TikTok is about the "superstars of tomorrow" – the newly-minted creators who have engaged with their fans to the tune of millions of engaged followers – the platform is also indebted to the bespoke and custom creators. These are the cosplayers, the trick-shot players, the artists, the jokers, the conspiracy theorists, the gamers, the magicians, the explorers – who post, share and like the work of others, all in the hope of expressing themselves in a way that engages with people who feel the same. And while many TikTokers find luck and followers with fame and fortune by going viral, ultimately, TikTok is about sharing your world with the rest of it. To its critics, TikTok may be "junk food television", but to its creators it's the beginning of a new revolution. Viva la TikTok!

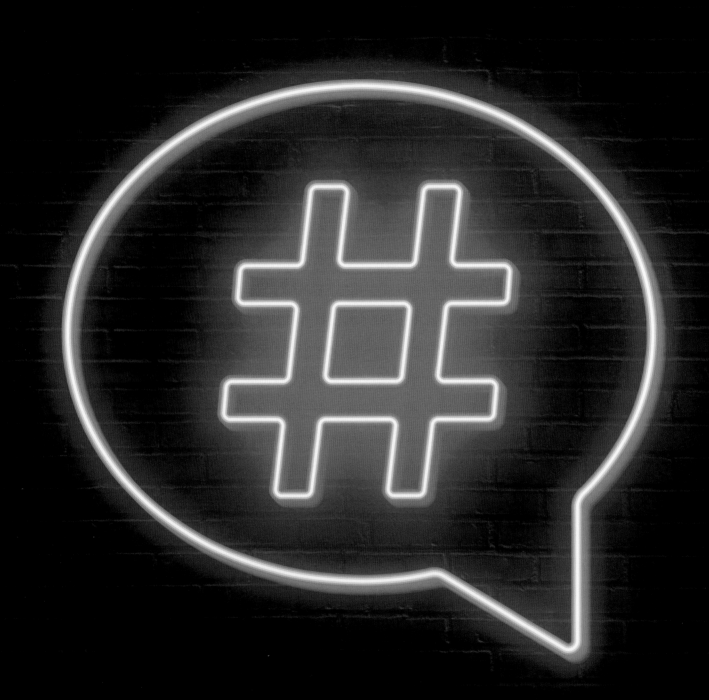

GET TO KNOW TIKTOK

IN 2016 TIKTOK ARRIVED ON THE SCENE, HAVING CHANGED ITS NAME FROM ITS PREVIOUS INCARNATION, MUSICAL.LY. IT WAS ONLY A MATTER OF MONTHS BEFORE THE APP CEMENTED ITSELF AS THE MOST POPULAR SOCIAL MEDIA PLATFORM ON THE PLANET. BUT TIKTOK ALSO GAVE RISE TO A NEW BREED OF SOCIAL MEDIA STARS – AND A NEW WAY OF COMMUNICATING. HERE ARE THE TOP TEN FACTS YOU NEED TO KNOW ABOUT TIKTOK.

ONE

In 2016, Chinese company Bytedance created TikTok out of the ashes of Musical.ly, a post-Vine lip-syncing app. TikTok then started as a Chinese project called Douyin (which is still the Chinese name of the app) and was then renamed for the global market in 2017 as TikTok. TikTok's founder Zhang Yiming's vision was to create an app where young people could hang out, and share their video creations. Today, Bytedance is now worth $75 billion, making it the most valuable start-up in the world.

TWO

As of May 2020, TikTok has more than 800 million active monthly users – and is growing rapidly. It is predicted that by autumn 2020, the platform will have more than a billion monthly users!

THREE

TikTok is popular all over the world, but the three largest nations with the most users are India (500 million), the USA (115 million) and China (180 million).

FOUR

An average TikTok user – not content creator – opens the TikTok app eight times per day and browses the FYP page for more than 50 minutes per day. This number is similar to figures for Facebook and Instagram, which means that TikTok has the right stuff to keep its users entertained!

FIVE

Approximately 70 per cent of TikTok users are aged between 16 and 24 years old. This makes the platform predominately used by Generation Z'ers – people aged 5 to 25 years old. Generation Z is the largest generation on earth. However, TikTok's users are ageing with the app – so expect more older viewers in the future, too.

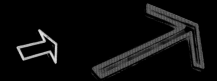

SIX

Today, a song that trends on TikTok also trends as a song on Spotify as well. So get writing some bangers and stick them on TikTok!

SEVEN

TikTok is real. Unlike Instagram, which perpetuates a false, perfect reality, TikTok is acclaimed for presenting life as it is – not how TikTokers would like others to view it. This makes TikTok the most truthful of all social media platforms.

EIGHT

TikTok's FYP – For You Page – is the "holy grail" for all creators to ensure their content is seen by strangers. It's wildly improbable you'll be a feature, unless you follow all the FYP rules which are:

1) Hashtag #FYP – USE IT!
2) Captions – keep it short, sweet and snappy (and ask a question or two to engage users!)
3) Use trending songs and sounds – the more popular the sound, the more users you engage!
4) Post when most users are active, i.e. not asleep, between 7–9am and 3–10pm.
5) Edit your videos – seamless loops, or effects – anything that makes your content worthy of repeat viewings!
6) Location – you'll see local content first.
7) Consistency – two posts a day – no more!
8) Duets – help create engagement; the more duets your video gets, the more followers you will gain.
9) New features and effects – use them when they are rolled out!
10) The shorter your video, the better. 10–15-second videos generally work best, as they are watched repeatedly and, most importantly, to the end!

The TikTok algorithm is very smart, but if you do all these things – you may actually feature on the FYP page!

NINE

Already, TikTok has been installed on smartphone devices more than two billion times! In March 2020 alone, the app was downloaded 115 million times, making TikTok the most downloaded app on the Apple App Store OF ALL TIME.

TEN

TikTok videos receive more than 17 billion views per month – that's 2.5 views for every human on earth! YouTube, TikTok's nearest competitor, receives only 15 billion views per month.

TIKTOK TOP 10: VIRAL VIDEOS 2019

These content creators went viral the most times in 2019:

1. Lil Nas X
2. Mariah Carey
3. Lizzo
4. Stunna Girl
5. Blanco Brown
6. Y2k & bbno$
7. KYLE
8. Luh Kel
9. **Billie Eilish**
10. Ashnikko

LOREN GRAY

@Lorengray

LOREN GRAY IS MORE THAN JUST HER MOVIE-STAR GOOD LOOKS. SHE IS A POLY-HYPHENATE: POP SINGER, ACTRESS, MODEL, DANCER, BEAUTY GURU, FASHIONISTA, ALL-ROUND ONLINE GODDESS.

In short, Loren Gray is one of the most-followed content creators on TikTok, with more than 40 million devout followers. Even though she grew up in sleepy Pottstown, Pennsylvania, USA, Loren was born to wake the world up.

In 2015, Loren joined TikTok when it was fledgling social media platform musical.ly. "When I started posting on musical.ly, I wasn't aware of what social media fame was; I was more interested in just making videos with my friends," Loren revealed. "But when I looked at my account after a couple of weeks, I noticed that a bunch of my videos had been featured. Suddenly, I had more than 30,000 followers!"

Since sharing her first dancing and singing videos, Loren has turned her TikTok into a hugely successful career. In March 2018, she signed a record deal and released her debut single "My Story" a few months later. Loren's music has been lapped up by her millions of fans who, naturally, call themselves Angels.

"It's what they are, to be fair", agrees Loren. "And I want my fans – my angels – to be able to approach me in public and not think that I'm some robot who only exists online. I'm a silly girl. I want to make stupid videos. I want to cry on the internet if I feel like it."

"I THINK THAT THE BIGGEST MISCONCEPTION, FOR ME, IS THAT PEOPLE THINK, 'OH, SHE'S JUST PRETTY.' IT BOTHERS ME TO THE CORE, BECAUSE THERE'S SO MUCH MORE TO ME THAN THAT."

ZACH KING

@zachking

AFTER CONQUERING YOUTUBE AND VINE, ZACH KING IS THE RIGHTFUL HEIR TO THE TIKTOK THRONE, COMBINING COMPUTER WIZARDRY WITH HIS "DIGITAL SLEIGHT OF HAND" SORCERY TO CREATE A PERSONA THAT IS SIMPLY MAGICAL.

Zach King is a world-class goofball. And, according to his mom and dad, he has always been "that odd kid in the corner with the video camera." It was while making his first short film when he was just an outgoing seven-year-old that Zach realized what he wanted to be when he grew up: a film director.

While a student, Zach decided to combine his knowledge of film technology with his own comic and dynamic creativity. "I thought, 'I can do special effects, I'm at film school' So, I made a pact with myself to post a video a day for 30 days and just see what happens. My first video took off, my second and third one were also popular, so I just

was like, 'I got the viral video bug in me' and just kept making them after that."

Zach first found online fame in 2011 when he posted a video entitled 'Jedi Kittens' to YouTube. The video was a massive viral sensation, and not only led to millions of views, but also gave Zach the confidence to follow his filmmaking dream for real.

Today, Zach's ultimate goal has been scored: he has been pursued by none other than the world's greatest filmmaker – Steven Spielberg – whose production company have bought the feature film rights to Zach's debut novel, *My Magical Life*.

CHARLI D'AMELIO

@charlidamelio

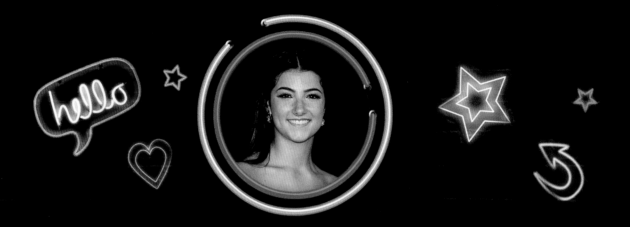

CHARLI D'AMELIO IS UNDOUBTEDLY THE QUEEN OF TIKTOK. TODAY, HER VIDEOS HAVE EARNED HER MORE THAN FOUR BILLION LIKES. THAT'S "BILLION" WITH A "B"!

Loved by her fans for her original choreography, as well as her funny montages and lip-syncs, Charli is the first to admit that she "doesn't understand the hype" about how she became so super-successful. But the reason is simple: her fans are just like her.

In June 2019, Charli D'Amelio posted her first clip – a 12-second lip-sync – to TikTok. Within three months, Charli was TikTok's most quickly ascending star, amassing hundreds of millions of views and hearts.

All of a sudden, the world was paying close attention to her choreography: a dream come true for this 15-year-old aspiring dancer who just wanted to meet Jennifer Lopez. Just as the insanity of Charli's insta-fame began to sink in, towards the end of 2019, she received a telephone call. It was her dream calling. She was invited to dance alongside Jennifer Lopez – her idol – for a TikTok challenge video to promote the NFL Super Bowl.

"When I first met her and I got to shake her hand, I was just blank face. I didn't know what to say. And then it kind of set in and tears just started rolling down my eyes because this was all I ever really, really wanted to experience and it happened and it was really, really crazy", she revealed.

"ALL OF THESE PEOPLE THAT SAY I INSPIRE THEM, OR I'M THE REASON THEY GOT INTO DANCE LESSONS. IT JUST MAKES EVERYTHING SO WORTH IT AND IT MAKES ME SO HAPPY THAT I CAN SAY I'M HELPING PEOPLE IN THE LITTLE WAY I AM. IT MEANS THE WORLD TO ME."

DIXIE D'AMELIO

@ dixiedamelio

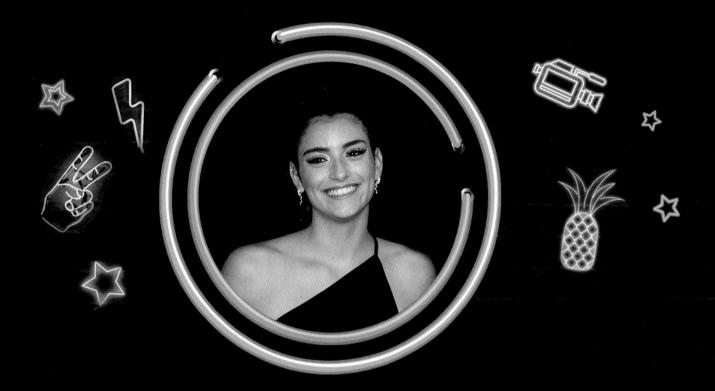

UNLIKE HER LITTLE SISTER CHARLI, WHO IS A TRAINED DANCER, DIXIE SIMPLY SHOWS OFF WHO SHE REALLY IS.

"I just try to show my personality, because I'm not a dancer, and a big portion of TikTok is dancing," Dixie has said. "Charli and I are two different people, and we've always tried to never be in competition. I don't want to do what she's doing. I don't want to be a dancer, because that's her thing and I have my thing."

Dixie's videos rely on a combination of her own self-created comedic skits, lip-syncing videos, and intimate personal revelations. "Being able to do comedy, or skits, or just talking on TikTok is kind of my lane and where I stay", she says of her own videos.

The D'Amelio sisters represent a shift in popular culture, with younger people no longer interested in traditional celebrities. For the Gen Z crowd, TikTok fame is a "real"-type fame based on relevance and relatability – two traits that Dixie has in spades. She is often cited as being "real" despite the huge level of fame her family enjoys.

"Sometimes when I go out in public and I see people looking at me, I forget", she said. "I'm like, 'Why are they staring at me? I'm so confused.' And then they come up and talk to me and have a conversation. I'm like, 'Oh, I didn't even know. I thought there was something on my face.'"

ADDISON RAE

@addisonre

ABSOLUTELY ADORABLE IN ALL FORMS, LOUISIANA'S ADDISON RAE EASTERLING IS ONE OF TIKTOK'S MOST BELOVED CREATORS, AMASSING MORE THAN 40 MILLION FOLLOWERS.

A competitive dancer since the age of six, and now a member of Los Angeles' Hype House, Addison's viral dances and hilarious meme videos have made her a household name (at least among Generation Z!). "When I first downloaded TikTok, it was kind of as a joke", Addison said in an interview. "I made a post and out of nowhere it got 93,000 likes and I was like 'Woah, I like this!' I kept going, whatever, and made videos with my mom and that was the main thing that blew up."

Addison got the idea to try TikTok for herself from children she babysat for – and now the app has changed her life forever. Pretty soon, Addison asked her mom, Sheri Easterling, to join in her TikToking and after her viral hit of Addison and her mom dancing to Mariah Carey's song "Obsessed" got the like of approval from Mariah Carey herself – an avid adorer of Tiktok – Addison's page blew up over night! Within six months, Addison had swapped Louisiana for Los Angeles. "I remember that's when it changed for me", she said. "I knew I wanted to take it more seriously and expand it to other platforms."

BABY ARIEL

@BabyAriel

WITH MORE THAN 30 MILLION FOLLOWERS, BABY ARIEL IS NOW ALL GROWN-UP ON TIKTOK.

Born Ariel Rebecca Martin in 2000, this beautiful and accomplished singer-actress is now one of the world's most famous people. In fact, in 2017, the prestigious *Time* magazine recognized Ariel as one of the most influential people on the internet. Of course, it's all lost on her. "I don't feel like I'm so influential. I still feel like I'm just a kid sharing my life and following my dreams."

Ariel's lip-syncing videos, dances, memes and sharing of precious family moments are lapped up by her fans, all eager to look inside her amazing and extraordinary life. But, despite the fame and internet superstardom, Ariel is the same today as

she has always been. "It's funny – I don't really think about it, like, keeping up with so many followers. I post the same way I would if it was just me, my family and close friends."

In 2019, Ariel made the leap to the small screen in *Bixler High Private Eye*, as well as publishing her dream-biography, *Dreaming Out Loud*, not to mention releasing more of her own music. Ariel dreams of future film-star success and has dreams of starring in a big-budget Hollywood movie (alongside her crush Timothée Chalamet) as well as collaborating with Billie Eilish. "How awesome would that be?!" she said. If anyone can do it, she can…

"I LOVE ACTING, SINGING, WRITING AND MAKING VIDEOS. THOSE ARE ALL THE THINGS I STILL WANT TO KEEP DOING."

KRISTEN HANCHER

@ k r i s t e n h a n c h e r

BEAUTIFUL. FUNNY. SASSY. TALENTED. THERE'S LITTLE WONDER HOW OR WHY CANADIAN KRISTEN HANCHER HAS AMASSED MORE THAN 23 MILLION FOLLOWERS.

There's so much about her to like and love. Kristen first found followers on musical.ly in 2015 by posting funny and inventive lip-synching videos. It then didn't take long for this creator to begin posting more involved videos about beauty, fitness, hair and makeup – the clips for which she is known the best. It was on 8 July 2019 that the Kristen TikTokers know and love now first glowed up on the platform. Kristen uploaded a video of herself recreating many of Kylie Jenner's Instagram photos. (The two do look strikingly alike!)

Over night, Kristen shot to fame. However, there is now so much more to Kristen than her Kylie similarities, and today she is one of the biggest beauty, hair-dressing and fitness gurus on the platform, often showcasing awesome and innovative beauty tips and a multitude of hairstyles – lots of new cuts and colourings! – with every new post. But, as always, Kristen's most important beauty advice is as simple as it is wise: "Embrace yourself, love others, and do what you want." Amen Kristen!

"EMBRACE YOURSELF, LOVE OTHERS, AND DO WHAT YOU WANT."

JACOB SARTORIUS

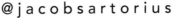

@jacobsartorius

ROLF JACOB SARTORIUS DOES, AND MEANS, SO MUCH MORE THAN HIS STRAPLINE: "I MAKE TUNES FOR YOUR EARS AND I LOVE CHOCOLATE MILK."

This plucky and incredibly lucky teenager – not yet 20 – is super-talented. Having begun his creative career at the age of seven when he joined a musical theatre group in his hometown of Tulsa, Oklahoma, RJS rose to internet fame in 2015, at age 13, when he began posting comedic and lip-synching videos on Vine, musical.ly and then TikTok. His sudden popularity led to the release of his debut single "Sweatshirt", which led to him becoming one of the most searched US musical artists of 2016.

Ever since, his has fame exploded. He has released several EPs, singles and travelled his home nation on headline concert tours. "I fell in love with just being able to connect with people. Just a couple simple words, add a couple notes in there and it becomes a song. To be able to sing and connect with people is pretty cool."

Today, Jacob's TikTok is action-packed with more than just music, posting hilarious memes and accounts of his adventures as an internet celebrity. He uses TikTok to show just how crazy his life has become. "I think that social media will be something that I always use throughout my career because that's where I started. You can't just forget about where you came from."

> **"IF ANYBODY WANTS TO GET TO KNOW ME BETTER, THEY CAN GO ON MY SOCIAL MEDIA. I THINK THAT'S WHERE I CONNECT WITH MY FANS THE STRONGEST. EVERYTHING THAT I DO, I TRY TO CONNECT WITH PEOPLE. THAT'S ALWAYS BEEN THE MAIN FOCUS."**

GILMHER CROES

@gilmhercroes

AS ONE QUARTER OF THE CROES BROTHERS, AND ONE HALF OF THE GILMHER–JAYDEN TWIN DOUBLE ACT, GILMHER CROES, AN ARUBAN TIKTOK AND YOUTUBE COMEDIAN, IS AN ABSOLUTE MUST-FOLLOW CREATOR.

Gilmher's life changed forever when, on 9 November 2015, he uploaded his first TikTok clip – his own unique homage to Drake's "Hotline Bling". Before TikTok, Gil was already receiving some attention for his acting in Aruba, winning Best Male Actor award at the Aruba Short Film Festival in 2015. That same year he was also awarded "Aruba's Social Media Star of 2015."

Gil decided to take an interest in social media when, at the age of 12, an unfortunate event occurred. "My dad lost his job when I was 12… that alone changed everything, I went from being spoiled to survival mode, fearing one day we might lose everything. That event shifted my whole life, I wasn't interested any more in finishing a higher education because my Dad did and he lost his job so I decided to pursue my dream of becoming an entrepreneur. Little did I know I was about to become world famous on an app!"

"I LOVE COLLABORATING WITH ANYONE. IT DOESN'T MATTER THE AMOUNT OF FOLLOWERS YOU HAVE. IF I LIKE YOUR CREATIVITY AND YOUR VIBE WE ARE GOOD TO GO!"

SWAGGY WOLFDOG

@swagrman

**THERE ARE MILLIONS OF ANIMALS TO FOLLOW ON TIKTOK –
WAY TOO MANY TO MENTION. HOWEVER, ONE DOG
THAT DESERVES A SPECIAL SHOUT OUT IS, OF COURSE,
SWAGGY WOLFDOG!**

A gorgeous male husky with famous neon pink ears, Swaggy is TikTok's most popular canine. And he has a lot of swagger to boot. With more than four million fans, Swaggy and his California-based handler Piper Rockelle (@swagrman) are the perfect duo for TikTok, offering fans tricks and insights into this special dog's celebrity lifestyle, as he hangs out with superstars such as Ariana Grande and Camila Cabello. Swaggy can often be seen dressed up and rocking different glamorous outfits, sunglasses and gear and his life looks as cool as it seems.

For his first ever video on TikTok, Swaggy performed the Justin Bieber song "What Do You Mean?" and, well, the rest is swaggy history! Go check it out!

"THE HARDER YOU WORK FOR SOMETHING, THE GREATER YOU WILL FEEL WHEN YOU ACHIEVE IT."

TIKTOK HOUSES

IN DECEMBER 2019, THE FIRST TIKTOK HOUSE – HYPE HOUSE IN LOS ANGELES – OPENED ITS DOORS. IT HAS SINCE BEEN FOLLOWED BY SEVERAL OTHERS. THESE HOUSES ARE A HOTBED FOR CREATIVE TIKTOKING TALENT, WITH INDIVIDUAL CREATORS ALL LIVING UNDER ONE, ALBEIT LARGE, ROOF, CREATING VIDEOS WITH ONE SINGULAR PURPOSE: TO GO VIRAL. WITH NEWS THAT EVEN MORE TIKTOK HOUSES WILL FOLLOW ALL OVER THE WORLD, TO DATE THESE ARE THE HOUSES BLOWING UP ON EVERYONE'S FYP.

SWAY HOUSE

Founded on 4 January 2020, the Sway House is a TikTok collective that homes some of the platform's biggest stars:

Josh Richards – @joshrichards
Anthony Reeves – @luvanthony
Kio Cyr – @kiocyrrr
Griffin Johnson – @imgriffinjohnson
Bryce Hall – @brycehall
Jaden Hossler – @jadenhossler

These six best friends all live together in the Sway House, a mansion in Bel Air, L.A., and churn out content as quickly as you can say TikTok. Founded by TalentX Entertainment, a talent development company that not only pays the rent but also represents other TikTokers including Alejandro Rosario, Joe Albanese, Max Dressler, Jason and Joe Waud, and Sarah Graysun, Sway House gives the boys a safe place to cause all sorts of mischief and trouble. Josh Richards, with 16 million followers, is the biggest star in the house, while Jaden Hossler, who joined TikTok three years after Josh, now has five million followers. As Josh said: "This is only the start of the journey and it's just going to get crazier!"

BYTE HOUSE

"The Byte House is full of love and positivity," said Jake Sweet AKA @surfaceLDN, referencing his new Honor Oak home in south-east London that he shares with Shauni Kibby, KT Franklin, Sebby Jon, Monty and Lily-Rose since the end of March 2020. These are the six biggest TikTok stars in the UK! "Originally the Byte House was inspired by Team 10, like Jake Paul's vibe," said Jake, speaking of the first YouTube creator house in L.A. "But now we're competing against the Hype House, country vs country. We're all super-productive, filming every single day. We're working together to become the biggest and the best… We essentially want to become the Hype House of the UK." Jake Sweet

> ## "TIKTOK IS A SUPERPOWER. EVERYONE IN THE HOUSE IS REACHING MILLIONS OF VIEWS. IT'S BEYOND CRAZY."
> ### JAKE SWEET

HYPE HOUSE

Established in December 2019, Los Angeles' Hype House is a humongous mansion hang-out hotspot and home to 21 of the biggest TikTok superstars on the planet. The Hype House was founded in 2019 by Chase Hudson, AKA LilHuddy, Thomas Petrou and Daisy "the peach" Keech. The full-time members of the Hype House are: Thomas Petrou; Chase Hudson; Ryland Storms; Charli and Dixie D'Amelio; Alex Warren; Connor Yates; Addison Rae; Patrick Huston; Nick Austin; Calvin Goldby; Wyatt Xavier; Hootie Hurley; Jack and James Wright; the Lopez Brothers; Avani Gregg; and Larray.

The idea for the house came from Chase and Thomas. "We both had the same idea," said Chase. "I was like, 'Oh, I've wanted to do this for months, years.' And he was like, 'Well, cool! I've finally found somebody that has the same desires and hopes and dreams in life. Let's make it happen.' And then we went out and did it."

As of May 2020, there have been some dramas and upsets within the house, with Daisy Keech leaving to set up her own house… the Clubhouse!

THE CLUBHOUSE

Established by former Hype House founder, Daisy Keech, and Abby Rao, the Clubhouse is the latest hotspot for young and famous TikTokers to create viral content as well as collaborate together on videos and brand marketing and promotion. The Clubhouse is a mansion located in Beverly Hills, Los Angeles, and by the looks of it (from videos the creators are posting), it's absolutely stunning. Residents of the Clubhouse include Daisy Keech, Abby Rao, Chase Keith, Kinsey Wolanski, Mariana Morais, and Leslie Golden.

JIFF POM

@jiffpom

WITHOUT DOUBT THE MOST FAMOUS DOG ON TIKTOK, WITH MORE THAN 20 MILLION FOLLOWERS (AND HUNDREDS OF MILLIONS OF LIKES), JIFF THE POMERANIAN IS AN ABSOLUTE SUPERSTAR.

BRENT RIVERA

@brentrivera

BORN IN HUNTINGTON BEACH, CALIFORNIA, IN 1998, BRENT RIVERA ALWAYS DREAMED OF BEING AN ENTERTAINER, HAVING STARTED ACTING AT THE AGE OF TEN.

Having first found fame starring in Katy Perry's two billion-viewed music video for the song "Dark Horse" in 2015, the super-cute canine has gone on to dominate all social platforms, including YouTube, Instagram and TikTok. With his awesome dress sense and ability to fit into all sorts of bags, boxes and glasses, Jiff is also one of the highest-paid earners on TikTok.

In between days on set, and creating scores of TikTok clips that showcase his unforgettable life, this fun fluffball is also a three-time Guinness World Record holder. In 2017, Jiff set the record for most Instagram followers by an animal, as well as being the fastest dog to run ten metres on hind legs and the fastest dog to run five metres on its front paws. But Jiff's awesomeness doesn't stop there: he is also the first dog to have its own day dedicated to it – yes, 20 August is Jiff Day in Los Angeles!

A decade later, he now has the TikTok universe at his fingertips. And with more than 25 million followers watching every frame of his incredible life, it won't be long before Brent makes it big on bigger screens, too. Actor, entertainer, entrepreneur, prankster, filmmaker, comedian, challenger, storyteller – Brent does it all, making his name as the "go to guy" for TikTok lols. He's also one of the big TikTok crushes – that face ticks all the boxes.

Brent's content, more often than not, relies on pranks and challenge videos, and often features other YouTube and Tiktok friends as well as his own family members. "For me, when I started making videos online, I was getting a lot of comments in person and online about being weird, and that's being bullied," said Brent of his humble TikTok origins. "But I stayed strong and stayed positive, and over time, my videos caught on."

LIZA KOSHY

@lizzza

ELIZABETH KOSHY, BORN MARCH 1996 AND ORIGINALLY FROM HOUSTON, IS ONE OF THE FUNNIEST COMEDIANS, ACTORS AND ENTERTAINERS ON TIKTOK. STOP WHATEVER YOU'RE DOING AND CHECK HER OUT!

She first began her career on Vine in 2013, before starting a YouTube channel and then TikTok – and today is one of the most inspiring and influential video content creators in the world. Not bad for a creator who almost didn't press play on her career. "The worst advice I've ever received was 'Don't post on YouTube, it's dying'," says Koshy. Thankfully she ignored the advice and uploaded her magic. "All of my opportunities came from YouTube!"

As Liza's comedy, camera and editing skills got better, it wasn't long before she produced and uploaded hilariously inventive and original comedy skits (involving all her own original characters), visual punnery, gags and parodies, that made her young fans roar with laughter.

But Liza's talents go far beyond the comedic. She can also do serious. In 2018, Liza sat down with former US President Barack Obama for an interview. He chose Liza and said this about her: "Young people are gonna be the people who make the biggest impact in this country, and you're doing a great job talking to them about some of the things you guys care about!" Right now, Liza currently has more than 20 million followers on TikTok, but come tomorrow she'll be president. You heard it here first.

"MY OFFICE IS BASICALLY MY PHONE."

SAVANNAH LABRANT

@ s a v v . l a b r a n t

**SAVANNAH ROSE LABRANT IS THE MATRIARCH OF
THE TIKTOK FAMOUS LABRANT FAM.**

Hailing from Orange County, California, the LaBrant clan – Everleigh Rose, Posie Rayne and Baby Boy LaBrant, along with husband and fellow TikToker Cole (from online comedy troupe Dem White Boyz) – are the first family of TikTok and YouTube. Savannah alone has more than 20 million followers.

While the entire LaBrant fam are natural born entertainers – in particular Everleigh – and showcase their perfect and wholesome family life in all manner of content online, it is Savannah who is the mom in charge. Her fashion vlogging has gone viral scores of times, as well as her makeup and hairstyle tutorials. Savannah's videos demonstrate her Christian values, beautiful family and parenting skills, often being viewed millions of times, despite being the object of a fair share of controversy in recent years. "The main thing we're trying to show our fans is a wholesome, not-perfect family that has a lot of fun together", says Cole LaBrant of his family. "God has given us this awesome platform that we use to glorify Him. We're having a lot of fun doing it."

"YOU MAY NOT UNDERSTAND WHAT GOD'S DOING IN YOUR LIFE RIGHT NOW... BUT JUST BE PATIENT, SOMEDAY YOU'LL UNDERSTAND."

KENZIE ZIEGLER

@mackenzieziegler

"DON'T TAKE MY TIKTOK SERIOUSLY!" SAYS DANCER, GYMNAST, SINGER, ACTRESS AND MODEL KENZIE ZIEGLER'S TIKTOK PAGE. BUT HER FANS DON'T SEEM TO BE TAKING HER ADVICE!

REBECCA ZAMOLO

@rebeccazamolo

WITH MORE THAN 13 MILLION FOLLOWERS AND 1.5 BILLION LIKES, REBECCA ZAMOLO IS AN INTERNET MEGA-STAR, INVENTIVE CONTENT CREATOR, INFLUENTIAL SOCIAL MARKETER, AWESOME ACTRESS, FUNNY PRANKSTER, INSPIRING HEALTH ACTIVIST AND FULL-TIME CREATIVE ENTREPRENEUR.

Born in June 2004, Mackenzie – or Kenzie as she is known – had already achieved a high level of fame before her TikTok and YouTube channels exploded, thanks to the TV show *Dance Moms*, on which she appeared with her sister, Maddie, for six years. Dancing and singing was just part of growing up in the creative Ziegler household; Kenzie started signing when she was six.

Despite her success, Kenzie's TikTok and YouTube followers keep her grounded. "Social media has made me really humble. I hate people who act differently because they have a lot of followers."

Today, Kenzie is also a celebrated author. Her first book, *Kenzie's Rules for Life*, is an anthology of life advice as well as an insight into the star's incredible life lived through a lens.

There is nothing she can't do, right? Along with her husband, and fellow TikToker, Matt Slays, Rebecca's *Game Master* videos on YouTube are brilliant – you must check them out. "I love making music, I love inspiring people and having fun. I am very aware of my audience and I'm trying to be a role model. Everyone has their own genius," she has said of her own creative inspiration when it comes to making her viral videos and TikTok clips.

Rebecca's internet fame took off shortly after she moved to Los Angeles in 2013 to pursue a career as an actor, model and comedian and landed a job in a comedic role on *The Late Late Show with Craig Ferguson*. Her success helped her launch her social media career and the rest is TikTok history.

AMELIA GETHING

@ameliagething

AMELIA GETHING IS NOT JUST THE FUTURE OF TIKTOK, BUT ALSO THE FUTURE OF BRITISH COMEDY. AND HER 7.3 MILLION FANS (AND COUNTING) WON'T DISAGREE AT ALL WITH THAT FACT.

Having gained a following with her comedic lip-sync videos when she first joined TikTok's predecessor, musical.ly, it didn't take long for Amelia to realize that she had so much more to offer her growing fan base. "When I was just doing musical.ly, it was purely just for fun, and I started to get followers from there really unexpectedly and obviously I was really happy about that, so I used it to start a career with. Fame happened by accident really," she said.

Amelia says her favourite kind of comedy is "random humour" and she is inspired by *Monty Python* and the *The Mighty Boosh*, but she takes her inspiration for all her YouTube and TikTok videos from her friends and family – when she has run out of ideas herself. Amelia's tip for TikTok success? "So many people think that you need a big budget to make good content but that's definitely not the case; when I first started out I had about £2.50 to my name and filmed everything in my bedroom. I didn't use sets or big fancy lights, just the light from my window if it was a sunny day, and I let my imagination do all the work!"

"I HONESTLY HAVE NO CLUE HOW PEOPLE FOUND MY CONTENT. I JUST POSTED WHAT I LIKED AND PEOPLE SEEMED TO ENJOY IT TO THE POINT WHERE I HAD A FAN BASE. IT'S VERY COOL BUT ALSO REALLY WEIRD WHEN YOU THINK ABOUT IT."

ZEPHAN CLARK

@zephanclak

WITH THREE MILLION FANS AND RISING, ZEPHAN CLARK IS A TIKTOK SUPERSTAR SENSATION SOON TO BE SEEN ON EVEN MORE SCREENS.

He first found success in his lip-sync videos to popular songs and has now transformed into a pure entertainment machine.

British-born Zephan is a social media star with a growing influence – with fans in both the UK, US and his now-native New Zealand (he is the nation's No.1 social media influencer). There's just one snag: coming up with new and exciting ideas based on his life loves: adventure, travelling and comedy. "I'm constantly thinking of new content to share," he has mentioned.

Zephan started his Instagram, YouTube and TikTok accounts as a way to express himself after a rough few years at school. "I got really badly bullied at school. But I didn't want to be all negative about it. So I went on social media and it became my outlet. I would take all the negative energy of being bullied and turn it into positive energy."

While Zephan is a hit across all of his social channels, it is his TikTok account that is currently blowing up more than even this young entrepreneur could ever imagine. "TikTok is what I'm biggest on", he told a radio interview. "Anyone can do it. Everyone should have TikTok because it's such a growing platform and its organic reach is absolutely insane... You can go viral so easily. You can do crazy things."

HOLLY H

@HollyH

WITH HER WONDERFUL, SELF-DEPRECATING GUERNSEY CHARM AND HER MULTI-TALENTED APPROACH TO SOCIAL MEDIA, IT'S ABSOLUTELY NO SURPRISE THAT HOLLY H HAS MORE THAN 16 MILLION FOLLOWERS – THE BIGGEST UK TIKTOK ACCOUNT BY MILES.

In fact, Holly H has even been described as the "most influential 23-year-old in Britain." First appearing on TikTok in 2017, after finding fame on Vine, Holly H quickly began to develop a huge fan base thanks to her comedic uploads that covered the whole range of TikTok trends: lip-syncs, acting, singing, and goofy dancing. For her legions of loyal fans – mostly from the US, UK, India, Germany and France – Holly H has become a new best friend and the big sister that every TikToker wants. Holly H, in her own words, describes her posts as "silly and fun".

"She was always a bit different," says Holly's mum, Jody. "She's never been wild. She loves watching Netflix and family things. She's quite weird, but she's always been comfortable with who she is. I think that's why she resonates with her fans. She makes them feel it's OK to be themselves."

In an interview with the BBC, Holly gave her top five tips to becoming an awesome TikTok user. Here they are:

Tip One: Be consistent.

Tip Two: Be yourself.

Tip Three: Don't listen to hate comments.

Tip Four: Stay safe on social media.

Tip Five: Have fun!

"I'M STRANGE ON THE INTERNET."

LILY-ROSE

@itslilyrose

PART OF A NEW GENERATION OF BRITISH TIKTOK TALENT, LILY-ROSE IS AIMING TO BREAK OUT ON THE GLOBAL SCENE.

One of the UK's hottest rising TikTok stars, and member of Byte House, the nation's first TikTok house, Lily Rose and her hilarious comedy, prank, meme and lip-syncing and dancing content is not to be missed by her squadron of more than one million (and counting!) global followers. From farting to spreading positivity to dressing like Spider-man to being hit in the face by footballs – to responding to the entire breadth of challenges, really – she tackles all the issues that matter in her truly original way.

As one of the biggest content influencers in the UK, Lily-Rose was invited to live in the Byte House in March 2020 along with her fellow TikTok creators – Surface, Shauni, KT Franklin and Monty Keates. "We had this idea for a long time – long before coronavirus," said Jake Sweet, AKA Surface. "The biggest influencers from the UK. We thought it would be good to move in together and create amazing content together."

> **"I ALWAYS SAY JUST TRY YOUR BEST AND DON'T EVER LET ANYONE TELL YOU THAT YOU CAN'T DO IT. ANYTHING IS POSSIBLE."**

TOP TIKTOK ARTISTS AND SONGS

ARTISTS, OLD AND NEW, ARE NOW USING TIKTOK'S ONE BILLION INFLUENCERS IN ORDER TO ENSURE THEIR LATEST SONGS AND ALBUMS BECOME MASSIVE HITS. A TRENDING TRACK ON TIKTOK EFFECTIVELY GUARANTEES A HIT SONG; AND AS MARIAH CAREY'S "OBSESSED" PROVED IN 2019, EVEN OLD CLASSICS CAN MAKE A COMEBACK ON TIKTOK AND PROPEL THEM BACK UP THE INTERNATIONAL CHARTS. THESE ARE THE BIG VIRAL SONGS, AND ARTISTS, OF 2020 – THE YEAR THAT MUSICIANS AND ARTISTS BEGAN TO USE TIKTOK AS NEVER BEFORE...

BENEE: "SUPALONELY"

New Zealander Benee's "Supalonely" became the first big viral hit of 2020 that literally everyone made a song and dance about. The track was recreated for dance tutorials, choreography (DC to Zoi Lerma for the choreography), lip-syncing, and all sorts of other madness, more than 12 million times. "It's completely wild!" Benee said of the TikTok success. "I have a little brother and he gave me the inside scoop about TikTok, 'cause I had no idea. He was like, 'there's this group called the Hype House and they're the main TikTokers.' There's this girl called Charlie D'Amelio and it was when someone sent me a video of her doing the dance, I was like 'damn, that's insane.' I searched the song and saw the people doing it and I was like 'oh my goodness.' These really young kids have millions of followers and I'm like 'oh crap they're all doing my song!'"

DRAKE: "NONSTOP" AND "TOOSIE SLIDE"

Drake is one of his generation's most influential musicians, so it comes as no surprise that many of his tracks find a home on TikTok. Most notably, in 2020, the "Flip the Switch" dance challenge, set to Drake's "Nonstop", and "Toosie Slide" (with its TikTok dance challenge invitation: "*It goes right foot up, left foot slide / Left foot up, right foot slide*") were recreated more than four million times combined. The "Flip the Switch" dance trend was particularly funny. It encouraged two people – usually a man and a woman (but not always!) – swapping clothes by flipping a light switch in sync with the song.

DUA LIPA: "DON'T START NOW"

Dua Lipa is one of the hottest artists currently blowing up all over the world. Her song "Don't Start Now" has more than five million TikTok recreations, including dance tutorials and lip-syncing, as well as some downright hilarious treatments – we're looking at you Gilmher Croes!

LIL NAS X: "OLD TOWN ROAD"

Perhaps the most famous example of TikTok's potential to turn a track into a hit was Lil Nas X's "Old Town Road". The rapper's original version went big on TikTok, when creators used it in their own videos and transformed themselves into cowboys and cowgirls. The song's success turned Lil Nas X from a college dropout into a wealthy superstar. "I should maybe be paying TikTok," he said of the app's help. "They really boosted the song."

THE WEEKND: "BLINDING LIGHTS"

With almost a million recreations, the #BlindingLights dance challenge of The Weeknd's "Blinding Lights" track became the hottest viral sensation of the first few months of 2020.

David Dobrik's recreation is perhaps the best, earning more than three million views. David's caption to the complicated dance routine simply read: "THIS TOOK ME 2 HOURS!! hahaha I suck!"

TIKTOK TOP TEN: VIRAL ARTISTS, 2020

1. Jason Derulo
2. Halsey
3. Justin Bieber
4. Doja Cat
5. Ke$ha
6. Lady Gaga
7. Powfu
8. Shakira
9. Harry Styles
10. Marshmello

Y2K & BBNO$: "LALALA"

"Did I really just forget that melody?" starts the intro of Y2K & bbno$'s super-viral TikTok video trend, which now boasts more than three million videos. While the track is too downbeat and lazy for a dance trend, the song itself is perfect for well-timed edits of other creators' snippets of their lives when the "Nah, da da dadadada nananana / Alright, da da dadadada" lyric jumps in. The song's creators asked some of their high-profile TikTok friends to promote the song by spray-painting cars. "We had the song viral before it even came out…" they said.

CAMERON DALLAS

@camerondallas

CAMERON DALLAS' TIKTOKS MAY ONLY LAST LESS THAN A MINUTE, BUT THIS TALENTED CALIFORNIAN CREATOR IS HERE TO STAY!

Having shot to fame in 2013 at the age of 19, with his prank-filled Vine videos, it wasn't long before Cameron turned to Instagram, Snapchat and YouTube to amass a huge following which today stands at more than 18 million fans … and counting!

Cameron's enduring popularity is all thanks to his relationship with his dedicated fan base. "I think the thing I'm most proud of is building a connection with people and being able to help them through things," Cameron has said. "Let's say someone's going through some crazy thing in their life, and they're looking for an out and something that's going to help them. Being able to be that thing is pretty amazing. Creating that connection with a fan is what it's all about for me."

Via his social channels, and by detailing his crazy life for all to see, Cameron is able to show his fans the real him, an intimate part of who he is, and that is what makes TikTok so interesting to the star as a creator. "I think we're really relatable to our fans and our friends anyway. Like we share a big part of our lives with them and they relate to that, too. So in a way they don't live the life that we live, but they see everything."

JAKE SWEET

@ s u r f a c e L D N

JAKE SWEET'S TIKTOK IS AS BRILLIANT AS HIS SURNAME SUGGESTS. AND, AS OF THE START OF 2020, JAKE IS USHERING IN A NEW ERA OF UK TIKTOKERS TAKING OVER THE WORLD.

Jake began posting to TikTok in November 2018 as a way of sharing viral videos, challenges and trends with his friends who were also on the app. Almost over night, out of nowhere, Jake's posts started to receive a lot of likes and even more views. Thousands of them. Jake was hooked.

Jake uses a wide range of content to appeal, attract and delight his more than five million fans. From weird and wonderful observations about his crazy TikTok life to ridiculous pranks on his mates to little comedy sketches that burst into his busy mind. And while much of Jake's content looks as if it comes easy and naturally to the charming and handsome creator, the truth is that making content look as good as he does takes time and skills. "I treat TikTok like a full-time job," he revealed. "I'm up at 9am every morning recording, often until midnight. A lot of people think being on social media is easy but I'm thinking all the time about what I can do to keep up with the game. That's how you become successful."

Jake's funniest and most famous prank – though there are a lot, to be fair – was when he filled his brother's duvet with popcorn: a task that took more than three hours to perfect. That's what you call dedication to the cause and thankfully the results looked hilarious!

"I THINK TIKTOK IS ONLY GOING TO GET BIGGER AND BETTER."

DAISY KEECH

@daisykeech

BEAUTIFUL. FUNNY. KIND. DAISY KEECH IS A PEACH. NOT TO MENTION A TRAILBLAZING TIKTOK ICON AT THAT.

Once the talk of the town over on Instagram, Daisy was so big as a social media influencer that, along with Chase Hudson and Thomas Petrou, she helped found LA's now iconic Hype House – the place where America's best and brightest TikTokers all come out to play. And while her relationships with Lil Huddy and Tommy are currently in a negative space – Daisy left the Hype House rather publicly at the end of 2019 after much drama had ensued – Daisy has found herself in even finer form and

has started her own house, named the Clubhouse, which will open its doors to a new wave of TikTokers in autumn 2020.

But before all that TikTok fame took over her life, beautiful blonde starlet – and one of the most in-demand content creators in Hollywood – Daisy found fame on Instagram. She was a fitness influencer, Instagram model and a YouTube health guru, posting videos all related to mind, body and spirit as well as how to achieve the "dream booty".

"[THE CLUBHOUSE] IS THE NEXT CHAPTER IN MY LIFE, AND I HOPE YOU GUYS ARE EXCITED FOR WHAT'S TO COME."

LARRAY

@larrayeeee

HE IS KNOWN TO HIS FELLOW HYPE HOUSEMATES, AND HIS TEN MILLION FOLLOWERS, AS LARRAY, BUT TO HIS DEAR OLD BELOVED NAN AND MUM HE'LL ALWAYS BE LARRI MERRITT.

SALICE ROSE

@officialsaliceros

ENTERING THE WORLD AS BOMBASTICALLY AS SHE DOES ON HER TIKTOKS, IN NOVEMBER 1994, SALICE ROSE WAS A RAY OF LATIN-AMERICAN SUNSHINE FROM THE MOMENT SHE OPENED THOSE AMAZING EYES.

Larray started his walk down the TikTok hall of fame when he made an hilarious satirical rap video called "First Place" – dressed in a bright red onesie, naturally – and posted it on YouTube. It blew up and spread like wildfire and today has more than 40 million views. With his original rap video, Larray had arrived, but his fame was cemented when he began to explore gaming videos too, adding another way to communicate and engage with his audience.

Larray is true to himself, and it's the reason why he's now considered a gay icon of not just TikTok but all Generation Z popular culture. "What made me start talking about being gay openly," Larray tells his TikTok fans, "was getting messages from people saying I helped them come out to their parents – and the fact that me going online and being myself can help people be themselves is just everything I could ever want in my life."

Sassy, funny, beautiful and compassionate – and with more tattoos than just about anyone else on TikTok – Salice has gained more than 15 million TikTok fans for being more than just an all-singing, all-dancing internet comedy sensation. Though she is also that too!

In 2019, Salice made TikTok headlines for her coming out story, in which she spoke the truth of her experiences of revealing to her fans she was gay. The clip has been viewed more than three million times to date. But while she is known for being upfront about her life experiences as a "troubled" teenager (and being kicked out of high school), she is also as well known for her family values, and, of course, her hilarious sense of comedic timing. Fans love Salice for her realness, honesty and, of course, her jaw-dropping hip-hop and belly dancing videos. One thing's for sure: this girl can move!

DOMINIC TOLIVER

@dominictoliver

AS HANDSOME AS HE IS TALENTED, AND HAILING FROM HOUSTON, TEXAS, LADIES AND GENTLEMEN, THERE'S ONLY MAN THAT FITS THAT DESCRIPTION IN THIS BOOK – IT'S DOMINIC TOLIVER!

TANA MONGEAU

@tanamongeau

OFTEN AFFECTIONATELY KNOWN AS GENERATION Z'S VERSION OF PARIS HILTON, TANA MONGEAU IS ONE OF THE MOST POPULAR TIKTOK AND YOUTUBE CELEBRITIES THE WORLD HAS EVER SEEN.

Dominic has been killing it with his online comedy sketches for several years, starting out on Vine first and honing his skills, before becoming mega-famous on TikTok and YouTube, where he currently has more than 20 million eyes all waiting to see what crazy comedic stuff he'll do next. Combining original raps with his own brand of wildly energetic style and humour, Dominic has made such a splash both with music and video content. Even Taylor Swift – yes, *the* Taylor Swift – asked him to appear in her "The Man" music video.

In just a short few years, Dominic has proved that he is the clown prince of online comedy, as well as amazing, if not ridiculous challenges – remember his #omgchallenge? – for which he takes great giggling delight in.

Despite her recent, and very public, break-up with fellow YouTube and TikTok superstar, Jake Paul, as well as a few other headline controversies, Tana continues to put on a brave face and post her wonderful clips on TikTok. Hailing from Las Vegas, and born in June 1998, this blonde bombshell kickstarted her internet fame with her "story time" videos on YouTube. These clips would describe Tana's crazy life off-screen. Pretty soon she had millions of followers.

Tana says: "I think coming online to millions of young, impressionable people and saying, 'I'm happy all the time and my life is perfect.' And building this ideal for you to envy my life because it's so perfect… is wrong. Everything I do online, as always, comes from trying to help others through my pain, or mistakes, or misfortune, even if it isn't pretty."

DAVID DOBRIK

@daviddobrik

DAVID DOBRIK IS, WITHOUT A DOUBT, ONE OF THE BIGGEST INTERNET CELEBRITIES ON THE PLANET. YOU MAY HAVE FIRST HEARD DAVID'S NAME THROUGH THE GREAT VINE, AND THEN YOUTUBE, BUT NOW HE'S ABSOLUTELY KILLING IT ON TIKTOK.

David arrived in the United States when he was six years old, emigrating with his family from Slovakia. After high school, David's parents gave him an ultimatum: either go to college or move out. David chose the latter and poured all of his blood, sweat and silliness into his social channels.

Moving to LA with his friends, at first David found being a fledgling social media influencer too much hard work – and he had no money to buy food or afford rent. "I just remember how scared we were," David said of those early days.

David persevered through the tough times and today – well, he's a household name. Inspiration to join TikTok came from a fellow famous TikToker. "I met Liza Koshy around that time and she was filming her vlogs and I really liked that it was a small camera and you could just record your whole day. That was so cool!"

David's top tip for TikTok fame? "Don't stop." David has posted three videos a week for the past four years, without taking a SINGLE break. The reason for this is simple: David knows his fame could be fleeting so he wants to make the most of it while he can.

"IF YOU'RE IN IT FOR THE MONEY, THERE IS NO WAY YOU WILL EVER MAKE IT! NEVER. THAT'S NOT GOING TO GET YOU THERE AT ALL. I JUST MADE FUN VIDEOS WITH MY FRIENDS. THAT'S THE KEY. ACTUALLY THAT'S NOT THE KEY. DON'T TAKE TIPS FROM ME. JUST GO DO YOU."

WENGIE

@wengie

YOU KNOW WENGIE. AND IF YOU DON'T, YOU SOON WILL. THIS FORMER YOUTUBE BEAUTY AND MAKEUP TUTORIAL STAR HAS NOW TURNED HER CONSIDERABLE TALENTS TO MUSIC, SINGING AND DANCING.

Wendy Ayche, or Wengie as she likes to be known, is a Chinese–Australian entertainer who now calls Los Angeles, California, her home. She hasn't always been famous, of course. Before turning to YouTube to transform her life into what she wanted it to be, Wengie was just a regular person with a day job. "Leaving my corporate job was one of the hardest decisions I've made, but one I've never regretted," Wengie said. "I was paid over six figures at the time and I was the youngest person I knew with that kind of salary so it wasn't like I was leaving a horrible job – in fact, I quite enjoyed it! But I've always wanted to

be my own boss and have always been drawn to be an entrepreneur… I was only able to do this because I was inspired by so many entrepreneurs before me."

After leaving this job, Wengie immediately turned to becoming a content creator.

"When I started making content, I made beauty and fitness videos because they were requested by my community, and after years of making content for my viewers I decided to do what I've always wanted to do for myself, which was music! The great thing about the internet is you have the freedom to make what you like."

AASHIKA BHATIA

@aashikabhatia

PREDICTED TO BE THE BIGGEST TIKTOK SUPERSTAR OF 2020 – WHILE ALREADY A BOLLYWOOD ACTRESS AND TV SUPERSTAR IN HER HOMELAND – AASHIKA BHATIA IS LEADING THE CHARGE FOR ALL OF HER FELLOW INDIAN TIKTOKERS.

Famous in India for her roles on Indian TV and her Bollywood film *Prem Ratan Dhan Payo*, Aashika joined TikTok to connect with her fans, whom she has come to call #Aashikians!

"TikTok offers me a great platform and I love keeping my fans entertained with the help of it," she has said. "In 2016, I came across this platform. I started to upload videos on it and my fans really liked them. It's really cool to be able to make fun videos and I'm glad for it. The love and support of my fans keeps me going."

More than just a talented actress, Aashika is also a dancer, a "muser" and pretty awesome lip-syncer, as well as a rather wonderful girlfriend to Roshan, a fellow TikToker with more than four million fans. Follow, support and say hello to Aashika now – because this time next year, she might be too busy being even more famous to reply.

"MY APPROACH TO TIKTOK IS TO LOOK AT WHATEVER IS TRENDING OR WHATEVER MY FAM LIKES. I CREATE VIDEOS ACCORDINGLY. MY GOAL IS TO KEEP MY FANS HAPPY AND ENTERTAINED AND TIKTOK ALLOWS ME TO DO THAT IN A FUN WAY. I OWE A LOT TO THIS COMMUNITY FOR KEEPING ME GOING."

TOP TIKTOK CELEBRITIES

THROUGH TIKTOK, THE VOICE OF THE PEOPLE CAN BE HEARD. AND THROUGH TIKTOK A NEW BREED OF CELEBRITIES HAS BEEN BORN. BUT THAT DOESN'T MEAN THAT THE CELEBRITIES OF OLD ARE NO LONGER REQUIRED. IN FACT, MANY OF THEM USE TIKTOK – AND ALL ITS CHALLENGES, SPECIAL EFFECTS, CRAZES AND TRENDS – TO INCREDIBLE EFFECT. HERE ARE A HANDFUL OF THE BEST CELEBRITY TIKTOK SUPERSTARS.

DWAYNE JOHNSON
@therock

Dwayne "The Rock" Johnson is an absolute monster on social media. His Insta and TikTok are always blowing up! With more than 24 million fans – half as many as Charli D'Amelio! – The Rock is the most followed movie-star celebrity on TikTok. His most famous clips are usually him insulting his best friend Kevin Hart, or pumping iron in his home gym.

SELENA GOMEZ
@selenagomez

With a whopping 18 million fans, Ms Gomez crushes it on TikTok, with one of the most high profile pages available. From promoting her new tunes to lip-syncing and dancing to her own songs or even using her hairbrush as a microphone (for singing), Selena will be one to watch on TikTok – as soon as she realizes she needs to post more often!

WILL SMITH
@willsmith

Will Smith is an absolute legend of cinema. He's a billion-dollar blockbuster machine. He's also one of the biggest superstars on TikTok, with more than 24 million followers. From duets with fans to special effects wizardry, as well as hanging out with other TikTok superstars such as incredible photographer @jordi.koalitic and Liza Koshy, Will do be good at TikTok, as the TikTokers say!

JASON DERULO
@jasonderulo

Keep this is a secret, but Jason Derulo is the clown prince of TikTok. His 21 million fans are treated to all sorts of goofy, ridiculous and hilarious content. As prolific on the platform as he is game to try all the latest trends, crazes and challenges – as well as being pretty nifty with the special effects – Jason may just be the one king to rule all of TikTok.

JOJO SIWA

@itsjojosiwa

WITH 23 MILLION TIKTOK FANS, "KID FRIENDLY" 17-YEAR-OLD JOJO SIWA IS MORE THAN JUST A CHILD SUPERSTAR – SHE'S NOW AN ENTERTAINMENT EMPIRE.

With her trademark glitter-and-sparkles outfit – as if a unicorn burst into life in human form – and forever-present glittery neon hair bow and ponytail, Jojo is without a doubt the cheeriest TikToker in the land, and her TikToks are pure rainbow-riding roller-coaster fun.

Alongside Kenzie Ziegler, Jojo came to fame via the long-running TV series, *Dance Moms*, in 2015. However, upon signing a mega-dollar deal with Nickelodeon, Jojo has since rapidly risen to steal the crown and become the princess of American kids' entertainment, with more pulling power and starshine than even Miley Cyrus could have imagined.

With her calming, composed and colourful nature, Jojo has lit up across all her social channels and is now no longer considered a former child TV star – she is a global brand. "I knew, obviously, that I wanted to be onstage, but I'm from Omaha, Nebraska. That doesn't really happen out there," said Jojo of her humble beginnings, and love of performance. After her TV and Nickelodeon presence had been established, JoJo turned to her fans on YouTube and TikTok to truly plot her course for world domination. "I never forget where I came from with YouTube. I wouldn't be where I am today without it. But it is a full-time job. You're filming all day, editing all night, creating thumbnails, keeping content fun and exciting."

"A LOT OF PEOPLE THINK THAT I'M FORCED INTO WEARING A HAIR BOW, AND FORCED TO DRESS HOW I DRESS, AND FORCED TO TALK HOW I TALK, AND FORCED TO PROMOTE THINGS THAT I PROMOTE. BUT THAT'S A WHOLE LOAD OF CUPCAKES AND UNICORNS."

NATHAN TRISKA

@ n a t h a n t r i s k a

NATHAN TRISKA BLEW UP ON SOCIAL MEDIA AS EARLY AS 2012, WHEN HE FIRST JOINED TWITTER. EVER SINCE THEN, NATHAN HAS MADE A LIFE OUT OF MAKING HIS MILLIONS OF FANS LOL.

It was in late 2015 that Nathan became a social media superstar, however, via musical.ly – which blossomed into TikTok. Born in Seattle, Washington in 2003, aspiring actor Nathan was encouraged to start making his living online when he saw the positive impact of other content creators on their followers. Ever since that revelation, Nathan's approach to making content has been simple: "Think of something that would be fun for you to make and for people to watch! Then, drink a lot of coffee and film it!" And his advice for anyone starting a TikTok channel is to "have fun, collaborate, and make them

consistently. Be yourself, and don't be too much of a trend follower. Set goals, and don't worry about what people will think; because people will love the real you."

Nathan makes four TikToks a day, a schedule which requires lots of time and preparation, including summoning the confidence to talk to the camera as, deep down, like a lot of TikTokers, Nathan is a shy and under-confident kid. "I have a phobia of talking to new people. Being a social media influencer, you would think I'm over this stage in my life, but I guess I'm still the shy 5-year-old I once was."

LAUREN GODWIN

@laurengodwin

WITH HER HILARIOUS SONG AND DANCE PARODIES, GOOFY PRANKS, LIVELY LIP-SYNCS AND COMEDIC CHARACTERS AND SKETCHES, LAUREN GODWIN HAS CARVED OUT HER OWN SPACE ON TIKTOK.

JALAIAH HARMON

@jalaiah

ATLANTA'S JALAIAH HARMON IS PERHAPS ONE OF TIKTOK'S MOST FAMOUS CREATORS AND DANCERS. DON'T BELIEVE US? CHECK OUT HER RENEGADE DANCE TO K CAMP'S "LOTTERY".

Hailing from Houston, Texas, Lauren started causing a stir on musical.ly in 2016. "When I was in high school I didn't have a lot of friends, but I had accounts online and mostly I had internet friends", recalled Lauren. "My friends through the internet told me about musical.ly."

Recently, Lauren has started to focus on her long-term social media strategy and has begun to build her brand as well as expand upon her acting skills, so that her content remains relevant, as well as to be found by a new, mature audience. "As my TikTok audience became older, I have moved up with my demographic. It used to be a lot more kids, but now it's more all ages. A lot more adults are starting to watch my content, which I really love."

Jalaiah's super-fly Renegade dance, like many that have come after it – we're looking at you, "Savage" dance! – blew up TikTok. The dance was created by the then 14-year-old Jalaiah. Unfortunately, as with many of the viral dance crazes, and the popular tutorials that spread like shockwaves through the platform, the original creator rarely gets attributed as its DC – dance choreographer – a big issue that content creators have on the platform. "I was excited and frustrated because other TikTokers weren't tagging me or giving me credit," Jalaiah said. Her frustration at creating something so popular – a dance that has been viewed, imitated, liked and shared more than a billion times – was disappointing, despite the fact that its popularity allowed Jalaiah and Charli D'Amelio to perform it together.

Jalaiah, who is now signed to super-star management United Artists, is able to show off even more of her skills, has moved on and looks forwards to creating more hella lit dances! "I really just want to be a choreographer", she says. "It's good that I influence other people, but I just like to dance."

Expect Jalaiah to be creating awesome content that blows up your #trending lists many more times in the months and years to come…

DANIELLE COHN

@daniellecohn

WHEN DANIELLE COHN WAS JUST 13 YEARS OLD, SHE TRAVELLED WITH HER FAMILY FROM HER HOME IN SUNNY ORLANDO, FLORIDA, TO THE FAST-PACED AND FRENETIC HUBBUB OF LOS ANGELES.

It was all in the hope that she could transform her tremendous TikTok and YouTube fame into her dream career: being a bona fide music superstar. Danielle hoped her million of fans (she now has more than 17 million!) would join her for the ride. Naturally, they couldn't wait.

Danielle wasn't an instant TikTok convert. "I didn't really like TikTok in the beginning, it was kind of dumb," she said. "But it wasn't about making videos. I thought it was cool to lip-sync to the songs, so I started doing it a lot."

Over the next few months, Danielle eventually shared so many lip-sync and singing clips that she quickly gained more than a million followers and more than two billion likes! Talk about WOW.

Today, Danielle continues to pursue modelling, acting and singing with the hope of becoming a global icon outside of the TikTok's social media bubble. But as ambitious and aspirational as Danielle is to become a household name, her main goals are much more inspirational. "I am very passionate about making our world a better place. I want to put an end to cyber-bullying and to help find research and cures for the children and people dealing with cancer." The world is all yours for the taking, Danielle. Take it!

"I STARTED TIKTOK AT A ROUGH TIME IN MY LIFE. SO I STARTED ON IT TO CLEAR MY MIND ... TIKTOK HAS CHANGED MY LIFE."

JAM=S CHARL=S

@jamescharles

NEW YORKER JAMES CHARLES IS, WITHOUT A DOUBT, ONE OF THE MOST AWESOME TIKTOKERS. HIS POPULARITY HIGHLIGHTS JUST HOW STRONGLY HIS PERSONALITY RESONATES WITH FELLOW TIKTOKERS.

Primarily a beauty, makeup and style influencer, James – with more than 15 million TikTok devotees – is as glamorous as he is gorgeous, and as trailblazing as he is inspirational. And his origins are as humble as his personality. "I used to do hair styling before I even thought about joining the makeup world. One of my close friends was late to her makeup appointment at a local counter and asked me to do her makeup before her school dance. I was like, yeah girl, but if you look awful, I'm not taking credit. Ha ha! It actually turned out awesome and she posted a picture. People loved it so I invested in a starter set of makeup to practise on friends and slowly began to build clientele. It wasn't until a few weeks after that I tried makeup on myself, and the rest is history!"

James' success (despite a few public controversies), has enabled him to become the first male spokesperson for a well-known cosmetic company as well as unarguably being one of TikTok's most followed gay superstars. In short: James is an icon.

"I LOVE BEING ABLE TO CREATE AWESOME LOOKS AND PUSH BOUNDARIES. I LOVE CLASSIC GLAM, BUT MY FAVOURITE PART ABOUT MAKEUP IS SEEING WHERE MY CRAZY MIND AND BLENDING BRUSH WILL TAKE ME NEXT."

JOEY KLAASEN

@joeyklaasen

FROM GREENWOOD, INDIANA, JOEY KLAASEN IS ON TIKTOK TO CAUSE ALL SORTS OF WONDERFUL TROUBLE FOR HIS 16 MILLION+ FANS.

Famed, revered and adored for his trick shots, athletic abilities and his comedic sketches and LOL skills, Joey's adorable antics are enough to keep his fans swiping all night.

"I started on TikTok because a couple of my friends were telling me to hop on it because it's 'the new wave of social media'. At that time I was going to go to college to study medical sciences, but I was like 'yeah sure why not'. So in my spare time, I would make videos that I thought were funny and one video blew up and that started it all. Most of my ideas would just come to me, but sometimes I would get inspiration from other TikTok videos."

These days, Joey lives in California with his musical brother – you might remember him from *The X Factor* in 2009 – to concentrate on his social media game as well as build up his influencer brand.

JONATHAN CHAVEZ

@paqjonathan69

JONATHAN CHAVEZ MIGHT JUST BE YOUR NEW BEST FRIEND. THIS RELATABLE COMEDIAN, SOCIAL MEDIA INFLUENCER AND CONTENT CREATOR FROM ARGENTINA IS LEADING THE FIELD FOR HISPANIC AND LATINO TIKTOKERS.

These nations combined could possibly become as popular as India and the United States – the two leading TikTok nations. "In the beginning, all my sketch ideas came from my mom," said Jonathan, "I actually started to make videos because my sister told me I impersonated my mom very well. I would do it when my mom would get mad at us. My sister said it was funny – that I should record myself doing it, but then I started to expand more into the Hispanic community because I wanted to make videos that almost every Latino could relate to."

With his witty and deadpan impressions, universal character creations and hilarious memes and life observations, Jonathan's follower counting is on the rise and will soon boast more than one million followers. "When my videos were being posted by big pages and started to reach millions of views, I got a lot of confidence because it meant people were actually liking them. I also felt very pressured to keep being funny."

As a rising star of TikTok, 2020 will be a very good year for this funny man.

MAHOGANY LOX

@mahoganylox

MAHOGANY LOX, AKA MAHOGANY GORDY, IS A DJ, DANCER, SINGER AND TALENT EXTRAORDINAIRE. IF YOU'VE NOT HEARD OF HER THEN YOU MUST BE TIKTOKING ALL WRONG.

Mahogany is the writer-singer behind many of the app's boldest and most original choreography. You'll know the "Take Your Man" song, and routine, for sure. It's a TikTok anthem! "Seeing "Take Your Man" take off like it did was surreal, I still can't believe it. I'm so thankful for everyone who showed it love!" she said of her first big hit and her first example of how TikTok can ignite a creator's career and spread it like wildfire.

World-beating music is in Mahogany's DNA. Her grandfather, Berry Gordy, was the founder of the iconic Motown records, the home of much African–American soul, blues and pop music.

TikTok's creativity helps keep Mahogany on her toes as a musician, and allows her to express her lyrics, music and choreography with immediate feedback. "TikTok is absolutely amazing for supporter engagement and creativity", Mahogany has said. "It also supports the music community for visibility and Spotify plays. TikTok has been a dream come true!"

The question is – how does Mahogany entertain so many millions of followers? "Honestly, I try to post at least once a day on each site, but usually more. As for which is my favourite… I'd have to say I love them all differently, but lately… I have been the most active on TikTok!"

MAX AND HARVEY MILLS

@maxandharvey

UK TV FANS WILL REMEMBER IDENTICAL TWINS MAX AND HARVEY MILLS FROM THEIR TIME ON THE CELEBRITY *X FACTOR* PROGRAMME IN 2019.

But for their TikTok fan base, now in excess of three million followers, Max and Harvey will always be adored for the short-form content they share everyday with their TikTok community, and as the rising stars of the "twinfluencer movement".

"Everyone loves music," says Harvey, detailing how he and his brother became so famous so quickly on TikTok. "So that was a good thing for us to have a talent in! And we caught on to the social media train just at the right time." But it wasn't just music that made superstars of Max and Harvey – their comedy skills, timing, pranks and observations keep TikTokers coming back for more. "That's just how we are in real life", says Max. "We have ridiculous humour as well."

"We started singing when we were about eight years old and have been singing with each other ever since," said Max. Aside from their continuing ascent to world (and TikTok) domination, the twins have just one path to glory: "To tour the world, to have met all of our fans, and to perform at the O2 arena." Big dreams certainly do come true for these two.

HOW TO BE TIKTOK FAMOUS

TIKTOK IS HOME TO THE FASTEST RISING NUMBER OF ONLINE CELEBRITIES – MORE THAN ANY OTHER SOCIAL MEDIA PLATFORM. MUSICIANS, MAGICIANS, DANCERS, ATHLETES – TIKTOK IS A BREEDING GROUND FOR ORDINARY PEOPLE TO SHOW OFF THEIR EXTRAORDINARY SKILLS IN THE HOPE OF BEING NOTICED. IF YOU WANT TO GET TIKTOK FAMOUS, USE OUR LIST OF ESSENTIAL TIPS BELOW. THEY WON'T GUARANTEE GLORY, BUT THEY'LL DEFINITELY HELP.

1. PICK A COOL NAME

Pick a username, or @TikTok handle that is original and memorable. Your full name is best, if possible, or a cool nickname that feels right for you and your content.

2. REGULAR POSTING

Analysts and experts believe that two posts a day (or three times a week) is key to becoming featured on FYP (and gaining maximum exposure, so don't just flood your account with garbage – be regular, and think about what you share).

3. BE CONSISTENT

Don't try and please everyone and try not to divert from the subjects and likes that make you special. Be consistent in your message, your voice and your style. Be you. And be pro-active about it.

4. PICK A LANE

What subject or theme defines what you want your TikTok to be? Gaming, comedy, art, trick shots, magic, lip-syncing, cosplaying, dancing, skincare tutorials? Pick a general theme that defines your content and what you are talented in. And develop that theme as a brand.

5. CONNECT!

Reach out and connect with other influencers and TikTok users who are sharing and posting the same content as you. Ask them for a collaboration, and advice on how to increase your follower count.

6. GO LIVE

Experiment with the "Live" feature – especially when hashtagging a beautiful or busy location or when you are with other TikTokers together. Try out all the new features that TikTok rolls out and be the first to go viral with it, too!

7. PICK A PARTNER

Ask other influencers whom you admire, or other TikTokers who share the same content, and invite them for duets and collaborations. The more the merrier. Piggyback on their followers.

8. DON'T TAKE IT SERIOUSLY

It's OK to re-create trends, or challenges, or lip-sync, or popular sounds or songs – no one will judge you for it, as long as you are being genuine. Participate in challenges using viral hashtags, which increase the chance of being seen and followed by TikTok users.

Don't take TikTok seriously – just enjoy doing what makes you happy. Whatever that may be…

9. USE EFFECTS

Try to be the first to use the scores of new and trending effects that TikTok rolls out, as well as using existing effects in a surprising or inventive way that perhaps no one else has thought of. If you do, other influencers will copy you.

10. HASHTAGS

Hashtags are vital on TikTok and are used more than on any other platform. With the right combination of hashtags, your videos could be seen by the right people at the right time, as well as used in TikTok's own FYP algorithm.

11. FOLLOW, FOLLOW, FOLLOW

Follow as many other users and influencers as possible. Be active in liking others and hopefully they will repay the favour. Also, follow the superstar influencers who lead the way in your special theme: if they search their hashtag and see your video – and love it – that's a bingo!

TIKTOK TOP TEN: SPECIAL EFFECTS, 2019

1. Face Zoom
2. Green Screen
3. Disco
4. Whirlpool
5. Portrait
6. Distorted
7. Fire Breath
8. Time Warp
9. Infinity Clones
10. Clown Makeup – remember Avani!

12. SHARE!

Link your TikToks to all your other social media platforms, in particular YouTube and Instagram. The more active you are on them, the more likely you are to collect followers.

13. LEAVE COMMENTS

Share the love of other influencers' and users' hard work by leaving comments if you liked the post and saying why. Your continued engagement with other users may lead to them returning the favour when they see your post.

14. THE THREE PS

Be patient. Persevere. And be positive. If you're enjoying creating and having fun, keep on doing it even if no one is watching. One day, you never know…

ANNIE LEBLANC

@annieleblanc

ALONG WITH HER SISTER HAYLEY, ANNIE LEBLANC HAS BEEN SERVING HER ONLINE FRIENDS, FANS AND FOLLOWERS A DELICIOUS TREAT OF WHOLESOME FAMILY FUN VIA HER YOUTUBE CHANNEL SINCE SHE WAS FOUR YEARS OLD!

Annie hails from America's state of Georgia. In her tenure on YouTube and now crushing it on TikTok, she has become one of the most inspirational child stars of the digital generation. But despite her unbelievable online fame – as a singer, actress and young businesswoman – one of the most important aspects of Annie's stardom is to be a positive role model for her fans as well as other social media users. "I try to make sure that the things I do leave a positive image for the younger generation to follow. Spreading positivity and inspiring younger kids is very important to me."

As one of the leading online spokespersons for her generation, Annie feels the responsibility of promoting self confidence and a healthy body image – in particular to teenage girl fans who look to TikTok as a standard of how they believe they should look, which is perhaps not very real. "Being a teenager is so hard, no matter who you are… I just feel like body confidence, self confidence and self love all really need to be more prominent. It's so hard especially with apps like TikTok. It's really hard."

"BELIEVE IT OR NOT, THERE ARE A LOT OF HOURS IN THE DAY. IF YOU REALLY FOCUS ON YOUR GOALS AND DREAMS AND USE AS MUCH OF THAT TIME AS POSSIBLE, YOU CAN ACCOMPLISH A LOT OF THINGS."

KEKE WILSON

@keke.janajah

> **"I LOVE MUSIC AND EXPRESSING MYSELF THROUGH DANCE, WHERE MY FACIAL EXPRESSIONS HAVE BECOME ONE OF MY SIGNATURES, AND I BELIEVE IT'S WHAT'S HELPED ME STAND OUT FROM OTHERS."**

So said Keke in an interview immediately following the triumphant TikTok success of her "Savage dance challenge". You know the one! Everyone on TikTok has shared their recreational or tutorial video of them doing it since the coronavirus pandemic of early 2020 meant everyone had to remain safe at home. The challenge has become the dance of TikTok to date.

As a new, young black content creator, Keke believes that it is her responsibility to inspire others to use TikTok to express their own creativity and imagination. This is not only as a way to connect with like-minded creators, but also to stop them from believing that they feel unheard, or rejected in their community or country. "Young black creators, we have to support each other and surround ourselves with positive people that know what they are talking about when it comes to this business because the window is open and we have to keep it pushing toward where we are trying to go," she said.

Ultimately, Keke just wants to dance and share her moves with as many fans, followers and friends as possible, in the hope that TikTok, and her other social channels, transform her passion for dancing into a sustainable career path. Keke danced her way into our hearts, and we can't wait to see what she does next…

CASH BAKER

@cash.baker

CASH BAKER AND HIS OLDER BROTHER MAVERICK ARE CURRENTLY KICKING UP QUITE A STORM ON TIKTOK.

And if you don't know who either of them are yet – go check them out and you'll see how incredible they are. They are among the hottest stars on the app right now.

Together with Maverick, Cash is an all-round entertainer – singer, dancer, social media influencer – with millions of followers, his social channels demanding some face time with the blonde star. As well as spreading wholesome Christian and family values, Cash also spreads hilarious clips of original pranks, self-observed comedic stunts and skits and wild, daring and sometimes eye-watering challenges.

Hailing from Tulsa, Oklahoma, this seventeen-year-old superstar went super viral in 2019 with a chewing gum swapping clip that was seen and shared by more than 23 million fans (trust us: it was as gross as it was funny), as well as many other multi-million-viewed clips. While Cash and Maverick have separate accounts, they mostly do many of their video clips together. In 2018, the brothers formed a band – "Cash and Maverick" – and kick-started their claim to world domination by releasing four singles – all of which became super-streamed hits on Spotify and YouTube. Go check out the songs "The Way You Move", "Young and Broken", "Whatever It Takes" and "Queen".

LUCA GALLONE

@lucagallone

LUCA GALLONE, FROM THE UK, IS ONE OF TIKTOK'S MANY MAGICIANS. BUT HE'S ALSO ONE OF THE GREATEST ILLUSIONISTS, MIND-READERS AND SLEIGHT-OF-HAND EXPERTS YOU'LL EVER SEE.

Though if you blink, you'll no doubt miss it! With more than eight million followers, Luca is continuing a trend for magicians to find a new voice and home online – and to become cool again.

First finding fame on television's *Britain's Got Talent* in 2016, Luca soon realized that in order to continue his magical path to greatness he must turn to TikTok. "Since going on *Britain's Got Talent* they have asked me back every year, but each time I've said no. I feel that social media is the way forward – it has certainly worked for me. For many young people today, television is dying out. They watch much more on social media than they do on TV."

Luca's first love of magic came from his Uncle Bruno when Luca was aged six. "He used to do things like produce a coin from behind his ear, it was all very intriguing for a child, and I wanted to learn how to do it myself. A year later, I got a magic set for Christmas and it was amazing." From then on, Luca devoted all of his time to the dark arts, learning his witchcraft, and becoming a magician that will one day rival his heroes, like David Copperfield. Luca is magic – so don't let him disappear!

"MINE IS A KIND OF COOL, MODERN, STREET MAGIC. I CAN READ YOUR MIND."

ADAM RAY OKAY

@adamrayokay

ADAM RAY OKAY, AKA ADAM MARTINEZ AKA ROSA IS ONE OF TIKTOK'S MOST HIGHLY PRAISED, AND PRIZED, ORIGINAL CREATORS. SIX MILLION FOLLOWERS ALL AGREE.

In 2016, Adam's comedy creation, Rosa, a beauty and makeup guru, came to be after Adam began scrolling TikTok's FYP ("For You Page") and saw a voice was missing. "I had downloaded the TikTok app and I was just scrolling, doing my thing. I wasn't really thinking of making my own content. And then I just got inspired by myself, my childhood growing up and, like you said, everybody knows this Rosa character and I felt that she had been forgotten about… So once I brought her back, everybody was just so familiar with her and that's why I felt she did really well. I was honestly shocked. Like I said, putting my first video up there, I didn't expect any of this to happen. So it made me feel good because I'm able to put my community out there like that, in a positive way."

With Rosa's plethora of hilarious catchphrases – "open your purse!" – as well as her relatability – even Rihanna is a fan – the character, and Adam, have a bright future ahead.

"The fact that Rosa's able to go worldwide and everybody just loves her and is able to get happiness out of it – I love it. My videos in the beginning were made to make people happy. So that's still what they're there for. They're not there for anything else."

"TIKTOK IS THE FUTURE OF COMEDY. IT GIVES YOU 60 SECONDS TO JUST BE EXACTLY WHO YOU WANT TO BE. AND PEOPLE ARE SO CREATIVE. IT'S JUST SO MUCH CONTENT THAT YOU CAN RELEASE IT TO SO MANY DIFFERENT CREATORS AND SO MANY DIFFERENT TALENTS. SO I FEEL LIKE TIKTOK IS FOR SURE THE FUTURE OF JUST EVERYTHING."

LUCAS AND MARCUS DOBRE

@dobretwins

LUCAS AND MARCUS DOBRE-MOFID ARE THE DOBRE TWINS, WHO ALONG WITH OLDER SIBLINGS, CYRUS AND DARIUS, FORM THE AWESOME FOURSOME, THE DOBRE BROTHERS.

This brotherhood produce some of YouTube's most fresh and famous content. But it is the twins on which we will focus here – as they're crushing it on TikTok!

This wickedly funny duo are worth every minute you spend in their zany company. Producing a plethora of video content, including skits centred on their sibling rivalry (and brotherly love) break-dancing and back-flipping, pranks, gymnastics, challenges, vlogs and creating original music, the twins are high-energy, in-your-face fun – and the most popular set of twinfluencers that are currently taking control of TikTok. In short: they're about to take over your life.

Lucas and Marcus' brothers are known for spreading their PG, family-friendly antics that never flop, as well as pranking their friends and their parents' cars (usually with slime or post-it notes), doing backflips in sync with music, and dressing up in all manners of outfits and costumes, usually to enthral their fans – but scaring the living hell out of each other!

"We like to show our unique personalities, and unique talents when it comes to dancing, gymnastics and comedy," says Marcus of their TikTok skills. "We all reflect our own strengths in each mission to be accomplished."

CHASE HUDSON

@lilhuddy

CHASE HUDSON, AKA LILHUDDY, IS NOT ONLY ONE OF THE MOST FOLLOWED TIKTOKERS ON EARTH, HE WAS ALSO ONE OF THE MASTERMINDS BEHIND THE HYPE HOUSE COLLECTIVE OF LOS ANGELES TIKTOKERS SET UP IN 2019.

As a role model to the legions of Generation Z'ers who look online to find inspiration and icons for their own lives, Chase is perhaps the biggest star in the sky. Born in Stockton, California, Chase created his YouTube channel precisely 16 years later, followed by his musical.ly page a few weeks after that. His desire to make video content began at school. "In seventh or eighth grade, I started having a passion for making videos. I was like, 'OK, maybe I could take a shot at this and see if girls like me.' I started posting content by myself and it got a lot of traction. I thought that was really cool."

Of course, now, Chase has found an audience of fellow TikTokers who relate and resonate with his content, as well as with the man himself. "I like making edgy content. I like looking cool. I like showing off my outfits and listening to dark music that goes along with it. My content really goes off what my mood is, whether it's happiness, sadness, or anything in between."

"AT THE END OF THE DAY, YOU WANT TO ACT LIKE YOURSELF, NOT SOMEBODY ELSE. MAKE IT YOU. MAKE IT AUTHENTIC."

ANNA O'BRIEN

@glitterandlazers

ANNA O'BRIEN, OR 'GLITTER + LAZERS', AS SHE IS MORE WELL-KNOWN ON TIKTOK, USES THE PLATFORM TO EXPRESS HER LOVE OF FASHION, BEAUTY AND HER PLUS-SIZE BODY.

From unboxing videos of her latest fashion/beauty discoveries to her vlogs confronting her haters and doubters, through to her own motivational exercise videos, Anna is a tour de force in promoting positive self-esteem, self-expression and living a life in technicolour… as well as incredible at telling her trolls where to go!

But perhaps Anna's LinkedIn profile – she is a businesswoman after all! – says it best about this style and lifestyle icon. "Anna O'Brien was born with a big mouth, big heart and big ideas. She shares her life, learning and fearless fashion sense daily as Glitter + Lazers. Once a side project, Glitter + Lazers has quickly grown to become a cornerstone in the motivational and fashion communities."

Apart from possessing undoubted fashion, lifestyle and business acumen, Anna is also a published author, with her first autobiography about her life online available now, titled *A Life*

Full of Glitter: A Guide to Positive Thinking, Self-Acceptance, and Finding Your Sparkle in a (Sometimes) Negative World.

> **"SOCIAL MEDIA CONTENT UP UNTIL NOW WAS ASPIRATIONAL, CREATED TO DRIVE US TO WANT TO ACHIEVE THE SAME LIFE, LOOK AND EXPERIENCE AS OTHERS. WITH TIKTOK, IT'S TRANSFORMATIONAL; IT'S ABOUT TAKING SOMETHING THAT ALREADY EXISTS AND RE-IMAGINING IT IN YOUR OWN UNIQUE VOICE."**

AVANI GREGG

@avani

AVANI GREGG HAS 20 MILLION TIKTOK FOLLOWERS. THOUGH BY THE TIME YOU READ THAT SENTENCE SHE PROBABLY HAS A FEW MILLION MORE. AND FOR GOOD REASON TOO.

If you're looking for a content creator who is breaking the mould, then look no further – Avani, as she is known, is the TikToker for you. She stands out from the FYP crowd and delivers her followers original makeup tutorials.

"I'm known for a clown check video that blew up," remembered Avani. The video of which she speaks – as you'll know if you're a fan – refers to a series of lip-sync videos Avani shared in which she wore super-realistic clown makeup complete with coloured contact lenses, glitter and pearls. Terrifying, for sure, but also hugely popular.

Following the sudden fame, Avani continued to produce her makeup clips and tutorials, as well as standard TikTok videos such as memes, lip-syncing and dancing. It is the makeup videos Avani loves the most, however, as they allow her to show off her skills and artistry.

"I'm taking on makeup more seriously now, for the TikTok videos. I have the IGTV videos that I'm starting with and then I'm going to move over to YouTube. So, it can slowly like become where I can make my own makeup line." For Avani, the sky's the limit.

"WE PUT OUR LIFE ALL ON THE INTERNET BECAUSE THAT'S WHAT EVERYONE WANTS TO SEE. BUT ONE LITTLE MISTAKE AND EVERYONE ATTACKS YOU FOR THAT."

EMILIA WHEATLEY

@lumpytoast

ONE OF THE UK'S FUNNIEST AND MOST ORIGINAL TIKTOKERS IS EMILIA WHEATLEY, AKA LUMPY TOAST. WITH MORE THAN 400,000 FOLLOWERS, EMILIA IS ON HER WAY TO BECOMING THE TOAST OF LONDON, AND NO DOUBT THE REST OF TIKTOK SOON ENOUGH.

In summer 2019, Emilia found she was bored with the clunky and old-school ways of expressing herself on social media. TikTok was the answer. "I chose TikTok as a platform to express myself because it's so easy to use and create videos on, along with the fact that the algorithm chooses videos and people that you'd be interested in and you find people who have similar interests and passions to you."

Today, Emilia, who has received more than 4.3 million likes so far, is currently studying musical theatre at school in London. But her dream is to one day perform in a West End show. However, for now this 15-year-old TikTok sensation is happy to create videos for her newfound audience, fellow TikTokers whom she calls friends. "I've made so many new cool friends because of TikTok, which I'm really grateful for," Emilia says, adding: "I love how diverse the app is and how you can do so much and how you have complete creative freedom."

FUTURE FAMOUS: STARS ON THE RISE!

THERE ARE MANY RISING STARS ON TIKTOK: QUITE LITERALLY ANY ONE OF THE BILLION USERS ON THE APP COULD BE THE NEXT BIG THING THAT MAKES YOUR LIFE COMPLETE. SO, WHY NOT SUPPORT YOUR FELLOW USERS AND INFLUENCERS AND GIVE THESE TIKTOKERS A LIKE, LOVE AND LEAVE A COMMENT? YOU NEVER KNOW, THEY MAY RE-PAY THE FAVOUR TO YOU ON YOUR WAY TO BECOMING TIKTOK'S NEXT BIGGEST AND BRIGHTEST SUPERSTAR!